PRINCESS GLORIARF

OVERCOMES SHYNESS

BY
MICHELLE LEE GRAHAM

Princess LoHart Overcomes Shyness

Editor: Alexa Tanen

Illustrator: Yelyzaveta Serdyuk

Format: Rocio Monroy

This book is Dedicated to my courageous daughter Lauren Hart (Lolo). May your self confidence and strength forever continue to shine!

Honorable Mention:

Mason Christopher, you are strong, loving and ambitious. May your life always be an example of God's goodness to others!

You have both brought my life fullness and joy!
Love, Mom

Once upon a time, in a faraway land, lived a beautiful young girl, named Princess LoHart.

4

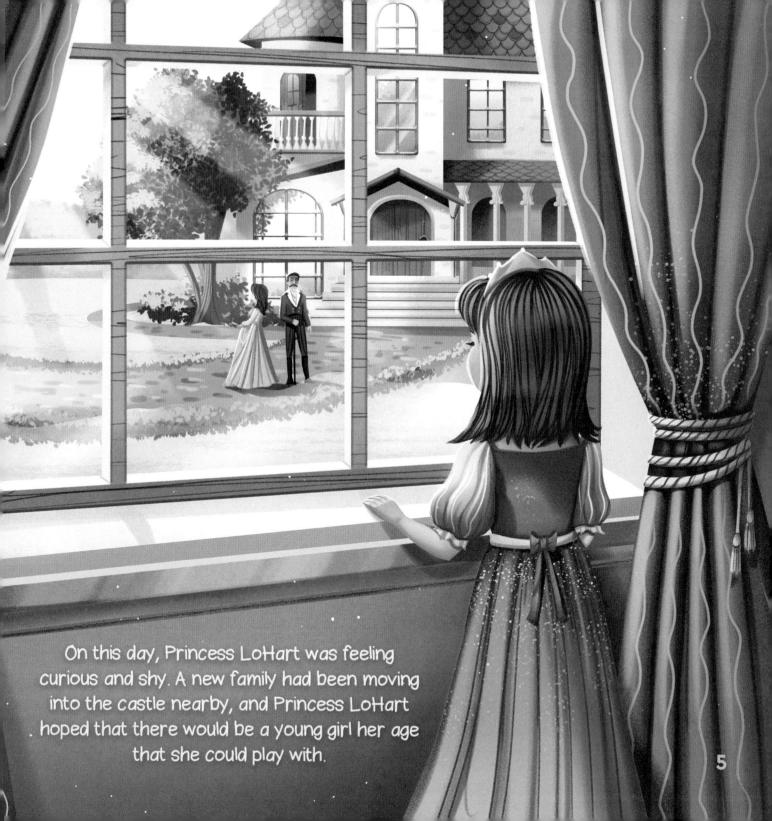

On this day, Princess LoHart was feeling curious and shy. A new family had been moving into the castle nearby, and Princess LoHart hoped that there would be a young girl her age that she could play with.

Although Princess LoHart had the whole castle to share with her brother, Prince Christopher, she often felt lonely and wanted another girl to play with.

6

The King and Queen both worked many hours and this meant that Princess LoHart had to find things to do for fun on her own.

Princess LoHart watched through her pink binoculars as the new family began moving into the castle next door. She saw stunning red couches, gold dressers, and majestic blue chairs. This was certainly furniture for royalty.

Unfortunately, there didn't seem to be anything for children. She watched for hours, hoping to get a glimpse of a new friend.

Finally, she saw exactly who she was hoping for! Another young girl walked into the castle carrying a stuffed toy. She looked a little scared as she approached her new large castle.

As much as Princess LoHart wanted to run right over and meet this new girl, she felt her tummy turn in a circle at the thought because she felt shy. She didn't remember ever feeling shy before.

After a long and disappointing pause, because she couldn't get her courage up, Princess LoHart decided that she should go find her brother, Prince Christopher.

Prince Christopher was excited that she wanted to play with him. Although she was initially not too excited to hang out with her younger brother, it wasn't long before the two of them got lost in their imagination.

3

They chased each other with bubble blowers, played
hide-and-seek,

and they really enjoyed a scavenger hunt,
looking for new amazing creatures,
shapes, and unusual things around
the castle grounds.

15

The following day, Princess LoHart thought again
about the young girl who moved into the castle nearby.
She wondered if she would want to be friends.

She almost had the courage
to walk over, but again
the shyness took over
and she felt her tummy
turn in another circle
at the thought.

Later that day, Prince Christopher popped into her room.

"Hey! I am heading over to the castle nearby, do you want to come?"

"What?"

She was surprised. She felt many new emotions, curiosity, excitement, and fear.

"Why are you going there?"

"I am going to meet my new best friend," he said with confidence. "I saw a boy my age and I am going to play with him."

19

He wasn't nervous, shy, or worried.
Princess LoHart was a little jealous.

"Ummm, I don't know
if I want to go," she replied,
feeling that now-familiar
turning in her tummy.

"Okay!"
And off he went to meet
his new best friend,
without a care in the world.

Princess LoHart felt terrible; she wanted to make new friends. She was sad that her tummy would turn every time she thought about it. Shyness was controlling her ability to make a new friend.

"Ugh!" She said out loud to herself.

"You need to be brave and just go meet this new friend."

She straightened her dress, smoothed out her hair, and took a deep breath, preparing to take a bold next step and walk to the nearby castle.

Suddenly she heard the ringing
of her castle doorbell.
Somebody was here!

Princess LoHart was surprised to see
Prince Christopher open the door.
Then she heard the voice of another young boy.

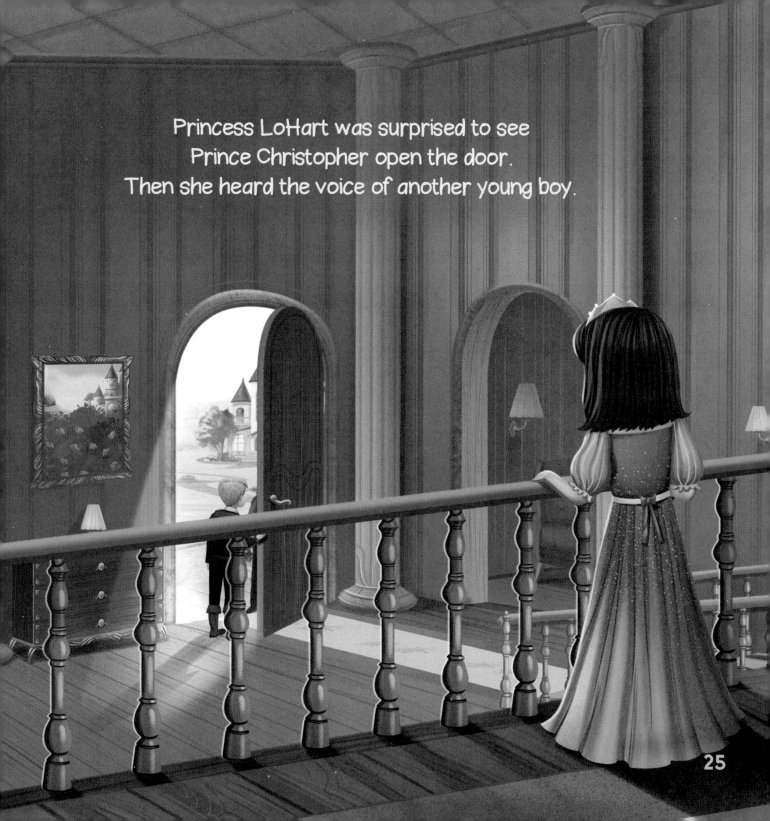

Princess LoHart
turned to walk back
toward her room with
her head down.

Suddenly, she heard a different voice,
a young girl about her age.

"Is your sister home?
I saw you outside playing yesterday
and I was hoping that I could join?"

27

Princess LoHart felt her tummy turn,
but this time it wasn't from shyness.
Instead, it was excitement.
She wanted to go play with them too.

She ran down the castle stairs
and joined the others at the doorway.

"I would love to play!"

29

For the next few hours Prince Christopher,
Princess LoHart, and their new best friends played together
and created new friendships that would last a lifetime.
This was only the beginning of their lives together.

As her mommy finished up the story for the night, Lauren smiled and snuggled deeper into her bed. She was excited to hear more about Princess LoHart's adventures and hoped that she could be brave like that too.

The next morning Lauren
jumped out of bed.
She was ready to start her day.

She was extra anxious to head off to school
and seemed more happy than usual as her mom
pulled up on the campus at her elementary school.

"Have a great day Lolo!" her mother called.

As Lauren walked into class, she felt her tummy turn, shyness trying to take over, but she remembered what Princess LoHart did.

34

Lauren straightened her shirt, smoothed her hair, and took a deep breath, trying to be brave. She walked over to the new girl in school.

"Hi, my name is Lauren. Do you want to play with me today?"

OTHER TITLES BY MICHELLE :

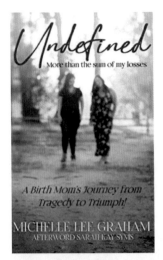

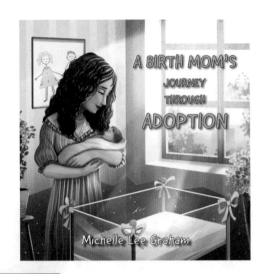

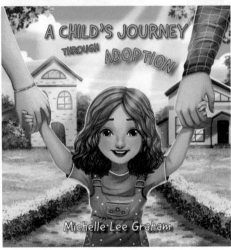

All books are available in Spanish

Available on

Scan the code to get your own copy

ABOUT THE AUTHOR

Michelle Lee Graham is a best-selling author, who has published four children's books, and an inspirational non-fiction novel about her personal journey as a birth mom. Michelle wholeheartedly embraces her role as Chief Executive Officer for a large non-profit in Santa Barbara, CA. She is proud to be a mom and grandmom. With over thirty years in early education and raising five children, Michelle has many creative and entertaining stories to share.

Michelle Lee Graham

http://michelleleegraham.com/

Made in the USA
Middletown, DE
09 September 2024

60651947R00022